INSIDE THE MIND OF A TEENAGE GIRL

Samaira Singh

Chennai • Bangalore

CLEVER FOX PUBLISHING
Chennai, India

Published by CLEVER FOX PUBLISHING 2024
Copyright © Samaira Singh 2024

All Rights Reserved.
ISBN: 978-93-67076-19-4

This book has been published with all reasonable efforts taken to make the material error-free after the consent of the author. No part of this book shall be used, reproduced in any manner whatsoever without written permission from the author, except in the case of brief quotations embodied in critical articles and reviews.

The Author of this book is solely responsible and liable for its content including but not limited to the views, representations, descriptions, statements, information, opinions and references ["Content"]. The Content of this book shall not constitute or be construed or deemed to reflect the opinion or expression of the Publisher or Editor. Neither the Publisher nor Editor endorse or approve the Content of this book or guarantee the reliability, accuracy or completeness of the Content published herein and do not make any representations or warranties of any kind, express or implied, including but not limited to the implied warranties of merchantability, fitness for a particular purpose. The Publisher and Editor shall not be liable whatsoever for any errors, omissions, whether such errors or omissions result from negligence, accident, or any other cause or claims for loss or damages of any kind, including without limitation, indirect or consequential loss or damage arising out of use, inability to use, or about the reliability, accuracy or sufficiency of the information contained in this book.

CONTENTS

1. Teenage Dream 1
2. Not All Men 3
3. To Love My Sickness 5
4. My Parents Child 7
5. Choices 11
6. Resist 13
7. All I Do Is Try 15
8. Roe's Redemption 17
9. Recovery 19
10. Object To Spare 21
11. 1 23
12. Sunflower 25
13. Pink 27
14. Believe Me 29
15. Staying Alive 31
16. I Am Better 33
17. The Teenage Girl 35
18. Growing 37
19. Moon 41

Contents

20. To Be Loved 43
21. I Care 45
22. Dreams And Daisies (Ridiculed Femininity) 49

"Oh how I love being a woman"

Teenage Dream

After the time passes, who will I be?
The time is ticking, each second feels greyer than the last
After the time passes, what will life be?
With the colour of youth leaving me surpassed

I'm sorry for being naïve
I'm sorry for being mature
I'm sorry for being too young
I'm sorry for being older than I should

I apologize for being in the interim
I know my novelty was integral

After the time passes, would they want me?
Would my bright eyes still lead them to reminisce?
After the time passes, would I want me?
Or would I just be another woman past her expiration date, lost in the abyss?

We're perishable property- an ornament of originality.

Inside the Mind of A Teenage Girl

I'm sorry for being grown
I'm sorry for being doe eyed
I'm sorry for being too young to understand
I'm sorry for being too old to not care
I apologize for growing old
I should know that is when my story stops getting told.

Not All Men

Not all men
But the fear that courses through my veins is all the same
Not all men
But the world hides a twisted game
A one in which ghosts of victims lie
And only privilege survives
Not all men
But this isn't a fantasy,
We live in actuality
Where human quality counts for none
But our bodies are the grand sum
Not all men
But I would rather mistake warning signs
Then fall victim to their lies
Not all men
But all we wish is to be seen
Because she was only seventeen.

To Love My Sickness

Sick love
Phases of all-encompassing guilt
The familiar ecstasy fits like a glove
Phases where even my own conscience will wilt

I love my sickness
From the depths of my heart
For times in pure quickness
A pleasure that forebodes a new start

How could I not fall?
If the fall was so sweet
The only pure joy that drugs my system occurs when
I am small
For when I starve, I feel complete

Concerned calls are no longer sirens on these days
Don't call me sick or I'll take it as praise

My Parents Child

My soul is getting weary
It's fate cemented in stone
Roots of my lineage sprout to consummate my theory
That the way I am is a familial loan

You say I have pretty eyes, I can't help but feel like that lie is tainted
My eyes are deep brown the colour of nothing but my family line
But then again pain is beauty and that's all my blood has painted.

I stand and look at my tree,
Its braches coiled around my neck
Years' worth of women trying to be free
And men with egos to wreck

You say you admire my empathy, I can't help but feel like that's backhanded
My empathy is consequence of moving past my family line

But then again agony births love and that's all they have left me with branded

My family line is all I own- a testament to my being
Its bumps and edges mould my varieties
And keep me stuck in blinded seeing
No I cannot run, so I fall to my knees

I cannot escape the wild
At the end of the day, I am my parent's child

Choices

You hear the sirens
You swear you saw the signs
The world you see crumbles in its lies
Hands turn to ice
Lips tremble with words of a heavy price
Outside it's summer
But she chills with what you've taken from her
My body my right
Until it's a uterus that puts up the fight

Resist

The air surrounding me stales
While I breathe in the smoke of the stories I hailed

When love is a promise and not an action
And their claims never gained traction
Asking questions like, "why are you like this? "
While learning how to resist

Resist the urge to reach out and forget
Resist their deadly game of roulette
Remember that they're the adult
And that no child should go through that

So I'll leave the hands that once helped me walk
And learn to run even if I fall

All I Do Is Try

You're not trying hard enough they say
With feigned disappointment and dismay
You lift up your head and keep your defence at bay
All you did was try

Still you work harder to make their pride stay
When work to the bone takes on a new meaning,
You crumble away
And still, you're not trying hard enough they say

So you set goals too far to reach
And unto your last hopes you leech
From skipping meals to skipping sleep,
You plead with them to see your health's breach
Still, you're not trying hard enough is all they preach

And one day you stop trying
To everyone else it will be horrifying
But to you it would just be satisfying.

I'm really tired of trying.

Roe's Redemption

Falls apart with just one nudge
The bricks in her wall withered from touch
Years of red spread across her wake
Still all she has is stripped away

Now she's in, in too deep
In hopes of a life better than her ancestors have seen
Her eyes stayed there in a shocked sleep
Because when she saw the news she was too tired to weep

Still she picks up her pieces and raises her sign up for roe
In hopes that she could meet her ancestors with rights they had 50 years ago

Recovery

When the fear of numbers weigh heavier than you
And scales have you all consumed
The only way to be healthy is to turn anew
And leave behind the path that you assumed

Try to make right the wrongs of your mind
And fight to find forgiveness from my body
Box the memories that revive and remind
Be the person you want to embody

Feel a day's breeze without feeling faint
Live to see another day
Numbers on the food packages won't be a restraint
Just a grave where my past self lay

To be or not to be sick is a decision I make
And I'm glad that it's one I decided to take

Object To Spare

Crowds loud, blaring
Your hands were overbearing
Hold me still with an iron fist
Thoughts of escape quicken to a list

Fear is fear all the same
Not lessened by a wealthy boy's game

If I was asking for it, when did I speak?
When I was silent or when I shrieked
But why do I care?
When I am just an object to spare

1

The wistful words of silence plead from me
Solace turned to dust
As I try to feign exemplary
Washing away my layers of crust

To reach my beating heart
Kept alive by mechanic whirls of webbed ways
As the only blood running through my veins turn tart
And the appearance of number 1 strays

An arena foiled to entertain my strain
I'm a spectacle of my worth
The praise runs straight to my brain
And covers the years of piled dirt

Still I set the curve, I invent it
And if I don't, I turn back to my silence and feel as much guilt as my gears can permit

Sunflower

Sunflower,
The sunshine watches while you breathe
And the faint pink of your cheek is all I can see
My breath hitches ever so slightly
And I wonder how the sun embodied
Is right by me

Sunflower,
It's the filled silence
The moment I knew
The only person who could turn me anew

It's the soft looks
Saved for only one
Nothing lasts forever, but I can't ever see
Me not loving you forever to be

Sunflower,
Please leave our memories saved in time
Losing them would be the biggest crime
You can see it with your eyes closed
I use your voice to find my home

Pink

Power,
How sane would you left if your power was not enough?
How sane is it for a mere colour to weigh the burden of a bluff?

Power,
I hated the colour pink, or did I?
Did I only view it through the guise of a guy?

Power,
Subdued feminism, fighting for rights only until too loud
When tension rises, hide behind the crowd

I never hated the colour pink
But only let my confidence in power sink

Believe Me

Believe me
For I have never been believed
Without shrouds of hurtful banter crashing around me like a sea
My youthful gaze misconceived

My truth is no less true
Because my hair skims past my shoulder
Yet it leaves men blue
And their fight to tear me down colder

I'm pleading to the wall
To you my femininity is a grave
I'm fighting centuries of silence to see these structures fall
But still to the world, I am a slave

To be a young woman means to fight to be heard
And to prepare for the silence even before it occurs

Staying Alive

Get out of bed. Throw away the dirt.
Fold your bed sheets and empty yesterday's thoughts onto the curb
Take a shower. Pick up the pencil.
Conceal the days past with a swipe of a painted stencil.
Smile at your neighbour. Be everybody's saviour.
Brush out the knots of past emotional misbehaviour.
Stay alive with any disguise. Even if it brings your demise.
Contacts will conceal the tired in your eyes.
Staying alive.
Staying alive.
Staying alive

I Am Better

Revive and remind
See the life come back into your eyes
Take your power back from the things that defined
Be the person that tries

I am a work in progress
Not a delusion of my mind
I am a work in progress
Not a person perfectly designed

This was not fate intertwined
Or the likes of something divine
This is my work I assigned
A necessity to be to myself benign

I am better, in a way not many people will see
I am better in a way that I feel free.

The Teenage Girl

The human clay
Moulded to peoples word
Through years of living through others way
Always keep your allure

Don't be absurd
Thirteen's not too young to be harassed
"She's a woman now" they slurred
Her clothes don't need to be a broadcast

And there she stays looking at the mountain of expectation
Say only what you have to, never out of bound
A script learnt word to word as a citation
And when the men are talking don't make a sound

Never in the right, always wrong
Where in the world can teenage girls belong?

Growing

I tentatively take the first step
A guarded silence that does not let my fears proceed
Brevity is the consequence of death,
 not life
And fear is a consequence of humanity,
 not cowardice

We're told to view the world through a cycle of hatred
One oh too simple to fall into blind
Acid leaks into the tendrils of what used to be sacred
And happiness becomes a figment of the mind

Until it's not.

I readily take the first step
A soothed power is all I'm met with to proceed
Strength is the consequence of me still breathing
Not a physical feat
Power is the consequence of my journey
Not the role I'm 'meant' to follow

Inside the Mind of A Teenage Girl

So as acid fights to seep into my thoughts I hold sublime
Viewing the world through a glass fully filled
Not afraid to grow and climb.

Moon

Looking to the moon and revelling in its sight
Its clichéd reverence described as nothing less than beauty
Marvelling its craters with no internal fight
But still looking in the mirror only out of duty

Embracing its dips and glowing lustre
But shying away from feeling the light
Taking all the power I can muster
To describe myself in a fragment of the moons manner
Disregarding it as vanity in spite

Seeing Jupiter as only a failed star
And yourself as only a cautionary tale
Still looking at the moon despite its scars
While letting your own stay at bay, stale

Our eyes aren't broken, we see beauty all around
They don't search for perfection, but bury its rules underground.

To Be Loved

What is a life without love?
When all its fleeting moments can only be sensationalized by its ideal
When love is gone, what is left to feel?

What is left without love?
When hate is a feeling too powerful to compare
Its intensity fit for the crown and not the spare

Because the pain that rivals love should not burn with any passion
To hate is to care, sparing no feelings to ration
It's just the same feeling re-fashioned.

I wonder if they hated me, the people responsible for my birth
They say they loved me for what it's worth
But the line is too hard to know
Both hate and love shining down on me with an incandescent glow

I Care

I throw the idea in a box of unmarked urges
I will not go there, I told myself I cared
I struggle through the desire to start again that my body purges
I cannot go back there, I swore I cared

My days of plagued sleep, squinting at package labels and staring at my body are over
right?
My days of falling to the floor, pinching at my skin and lying about breakfast to my sister are over
right?

I open up the box, the idea welcomes me
A sick smile on its right and on the left, a world of 'not having to try anymore'
I take three deep breaths in and picture where I should be
Nothing is working, I feel it to my core.

I worked hard to be here.

It's a twisted love, I say "I'm doing the best I ever have" through a tear.

Nothing will ever feel like that I fear.

Dreams And Daisies
(Ridiculed Femininity)

When dreams and daisies are told to decease
Whispers of girlhood adolescence are told to lay
All that's left is a lifelong lease
And lists of regret –
An ode to the good ole days

Dreams and daisies
Butterflies and breakfast
Giggles and fluttered feet all lead to me

And then tension rises
Regret turns to ruin
Years of sweat and tears amount to no prizes
And realizations of shattered secrets fill the place you grew in

Flowers and forget me not's
 Proposals and pink skies
Tulips and theatre -It all leads to me

Inside the Mind of A Teenage Girl

The fight we put up to protect our daughters and honour our mothers are dolled up intricacies
- A spectacle of rebellion
My dreams and daisies all lead to me
A grave of ridiculed femininity

www.ingramcontent.com/pod-product-compliance
Lightning Source LLC
LaVergne TN
LVHW070940070526
838199LV00039B/725